# GHOSTS OF GRAINGER TOWN

## Further Tales from Newcastle's Darker Side

## Vanessa Histon

Tyne Bridge Publishing

Acknowledgments:

I would like to thank the following people who were generous in sharing their advice, ideas and experiences:
Pat Ayre; Brian Bennison; Pat Blue; Agnes & Dennis Chilton; George Coils; Linda Conlon; Michael Cornish; Jimmy Donald; Christopher Goulding; Emma Gribbin; Norma Finlinson; Liz Harrison; Mike Hodgson; Ian Jackson; Sarah Lagun; Julie Lloyd; Chris Mabbott; Frank Manders; Norman McCord; Paul McDonald; Denise Patterson; Jenn Robson; Ken Smith; Laura Thwaites; Ann Walton; Helen Watson; Liz, Carol, Heather, Brian and Margaret from Windows.

I would also like to thank the Local Studies Section at Newcastle City Library, and Anna Flowers and Shawn Fairless at Tyne Bridge Publishing for their encouragement and support.

Photographs and other illustrations © Newcastle Libraries & Information Service unless otherwise indicated.

A catalogue record for this book is available from the British Library.

ISBN: 1857951263

Published by
City of Newcastle upon Tyne
Education & Libraries Directorate
Newcastle Libraries & Information Service
Tyne Bridge Publishing
2001

www.newcastle.gov.uk/tynebridgepublishing
Printed by Statex Colourprint, Newcastle upon Tyne

Front cover: Grainger Street c.1900.

# INTRODUCTION

*N*ightmare on Grey Street, my first book, was published on Halloween 2000. It explored traditional and long-established ghost stories and macabre tales from Newcastle's history. I was gratified by the amount of attention the book received. As soon as it reached the shops, people started to come forward to tell me about their own ghostly experiences.

At around the same time, my attention was drawn to an unusual and grisly item in the Local Studies Collection of Newcastle City Library. It is a book containing the skin of a supposed murderer. I was so appalled at his fate that I decided to re-examine his case, and discovered that Justice, for him at least, was not very just.

I have long been fascinated by the Victorians' obsession with spiritualism, and when I discovered that two of America's most celebrated mediums sold out venues in Newcastle on several occasions, I realised that I had enough material for another book.

Most of the buildings featured here are shops, pubs and offices – not the sort of places normally known for their haunted atmosphere. The people who described their experiences are not professional ghost hunters, but ordinary people who were usually concentrating on their work when they noticed that something wasn't quite right …

# CONTENTS

The old Infirmary on Forth Banks, pre 1906 when patients were removed to the new Royal Victoria Infirmary. It was finally demolished in 1954. In 1852 John Dobson contributed a new wing to the hospital to accommodate cholera and typhus victims. Due to be completed in 1855, it actually received its first patients a year earlier, when it opened to treat victims of the great fire of 1854. The operating theatre was unchanged from its original construction in the 1770s and infections were rife until the introduction of antiseptic surgery in the 1880s.

*Jimmy Forsyth*

The market house is now restored, and perhaps this has placated the ghosts, as there seem to be no more disturbances there. Photographed in 1994.

# HOSPITAL HAUNTINGS

### IN THE MIDST OF [THE CENTRE FOR] LIFE

The Centre for Life, one of the most modern buildings in the city, stands on the site of two much older institutions, the Cattle Market and the Infirmary.

The Infirmary was Newcastle's first hospital for infectious diseases. It opened on 8 October, 1773, in purpose-built premises on Forth Banks. The cost – £3,697 – was raised by public subscription. Nursing care was rudimentary and more able-bodied patients were expected to look after their bed ridden companions. Although there were 90 beds, overcrowding was always a problem. Shared beds were common, and it was not unusual for a patient with healthy skin to be put into bed with someone with an unpleasant and infectious skin disease.

The only old building remaining on the Centre for Life complex is the market house, built in 1831 by John Dobson as a toll house and office for the cattle market.

When the site was being cleared for building the Centre for Life, contractors knew they would find some human remains. What they weren't prepared for was the sheer number of bodies interred there. The bones of around 1,000 people were excavated. They weren't buried in coffins, but simply wrapped in shrouds. Many of them were too poor to afford better. Others were seamen, whose ships had called in at the port, off-loaded the sick, and then sailed away without them.

Most of the people had died, not of exotic diseases, but of commonplace things like infected boils. Many were young. The average age was around 40.

These people might have been poor, their lives might have been short and sad, but it seemed that something was watching over their last resting place. During the excavation, the old market house at the centre of the site became very cold, there was an uncomfortable atmosphere, and and things left there mysteriously disappeared. Security guards had eerie experiences.

Some of the bones were sent to the University of Sheffield for analysis, others were re-buried. All were treated with respect. This must have satisfied whatever force was protecting the place, because when the excavation finished, all disturbances ceased.

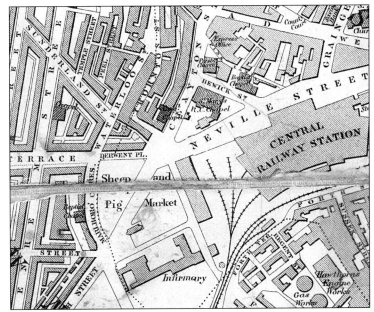

*From Reid's plan of Newcastle and Gateshead, 1878.*

## THINGS GOING BUMP AT THE BEEB

Having a baby in the 18th century was, for many women, a death sentence. Poor hygiene and sanitation, combined with lack of medical knowledge meant that many mothers and babies did not survive childbirth. Poor women, in crowded, insanitary housing, were particularly at risk. In 1760 the charitably-minded of Newcastle contributed to a fund to ease the situation. Their subscriptions paid for a house on Rosemary Lane, next to St John's Church on Westgate Road, which became the Lying-In Hospital and Outdoor Charity for Poor Married Women. Unmarried pregnant women were not provided for, as the charity's benefactors would not be seen to condone something they viewed as immoral behaviour.

Around 3,500 patients received care at the original Lying-In Hospital, but by the early 19th century, the hospital had outgrown its premises. In 1819 a fund for a new Lying-In

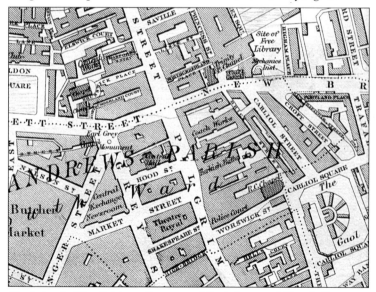

*The Lying-In Hospital is on the corner of Croft Street and New Bridge Street, opposite the site of the Free Library. It is now restored, and no phenomena have been observed recently.*

Hospital was set up. Land was acquired on the corner of Croft Street and New Bridge Street, and Newcastle's best-known architect, John Dobson, agreed to waive his fee for designing the new building. The hospital was built directly across the street from Dobson's own home which can still be seen as part of the fascia of a nightclub.

The new Lying-In Hospital opened on 4 October, 1826. It had cost £1,500 to build. On admission, each patient had to produce her marriage certificate and a child's dress. The homeless and those suffering from contagious diseases were not admitted.

After less than 100 years, the hospital was hopelessly overcrowded and the building was showing severe wear and tear. There were large cracks in the walls, and the staircase and landing were in a dangerous state of repair. Even so, over 1,000 mothers a year were admitted to this alarmingly unhygienic institution. In October 1923, the hospital moved to the Princess Mary Maternity Hospital on Jubilee Road.

The building lay empty for two years, then was leased to

the BBC for use as studios and offices. Although the building was in a bad state, it was something of a step-up for the BBC. Only three years previously the Corporation had made its first radio broadcast from Newcastle from the back of a lorry in the stables of the Co-op warehouse in Blandford Street. This extraordinary broadcasting feat was made necessary because of a technical hitch. On the evening planned for the first broadcast, 23 December, 1922, the sound line between the BBC studio in Eldon Square and the transmitter in Blandford Street failed. The only way the show could go on was for the broadcasters to work as close to the transmitter as possible. Despite extremely trying conditions, the first broadcast was a great success, although the piano music originally planned had to be cut, simply because the piano could not be wheeled across the cobbles of the stable yard.

*The Lying-In Hospital c.1923, just before it was leased to the BBC. The sign says 'FOR SALE'.*

Eventually, the link from the transmitter to Eldon Square was restored, but in a very short time the radio station outgrew this studio. The new Broadcasting House on New Bridge Street was officially opened on 23 December 1925, exactly three years after the first extraordinary broadcast from Blandford Street.

Over the years, Broadcasting House was modified, facilities were improved, and eventually a TV studio was built. But despite the introduction of 20th century technology, the building still retained some of its former character, and, apparently, one of its former occupants.

Engineers, who often worked in the dead of night, reported strange sensations. One stood in amazement listening to footsteps walking the length of a totally empty corridor. He was even more astonished when he realised that, although the corridor was fully carpeted, he could hear hard heels walking on a stone floor. A colleague had made a full tour of the building after broadcasting had finished one night, checking that everyone had left and the doors were secure. His last task was to adjust the clock in the control room. As he did so, he heard someone enter through the door behind him. He turned to ask them how they had got in, only to realise that there was no one there. Staff called the intruder the White Lady, and most thought she was the spirit of a nurse or a mother from the old Lying-In Hospital.

There were other strange phenomena in Broadcasting House. One announcer read the news on Burns Night to the accompaniment of ghostly bagpipes. The source of the music was never traced. An engineer, working over Christmas, was kept company by a ghostly cat.

In January 1988 the BBC finally left New Bridge Street for purpose-built studios in Fenham. The old Lying-In Hospital is now part of the head office of the Newcastle Building Society. During redevelopment, the old building was completely gutted and it is now part of the executive suite which is not in constant use. No ghosts have been seen or heard there in recent years.

*The Dental Hospital was built on land facing Framlington Place, shown here c.1910. Perhaps a friendly housekeeper from these well-to-do houses is the presence. This old plate is cracked.*

## THE PHANTOM DENTAL NURSE

Newcastle's dental hospital is a modern building, built in 1977 on open land. During the late 1980s and early 1990s, there were some strange happenings in one of the clinical areas of the hospital. One day a porter heard footsteps following him along a corridor. He turned to see who was behind him, but there was no one there. On another occasion a member of staff was working outside normal hours. He thought he was alone in that part of the building, so was amazed to hear footsteps on the floor above him. He went back to the porter's lodge to see if anyone else had signed in. No-one had. The porter came with him to see if there was an intruder in the hospital, but there was nobody else in that part of the building.

Whatever the presence was, it tried to be helpful. Each evening, the dental instruments were put away, but when staff arrived to start work the next morning, the instruments would sometimes be laid out ready for use.

# FALLEN WOMEN

## THE SERVANT'S SHAME

The Central Arcade, occupying a triangle between Grey Street, Grainger Street and Market Street, is one of the most elegant shopping areas in Newcastle. It was built by Richard Grainger and completed in 1838. Although originally designed as a corn exchange, the town's authorities and merchants would not accept it, even when it was offered as a free gift, so for many years it had a chequered history as a news room with an area for exhibitions. In 1867 it was almost destroyed by fire and was rebuilt as a reading room, art gallery and concert hall. The idea proved unpopular and in 1869 it closed through lack of support.

In 1870, T.P. Barkas and T.H. Twedy leased the building and re opened it as a combined news room, art gallery and commercial exhibition. The partnership must have been more commercially astute than previous

*The Central Exchange newsroom c.1860, before the fire of 1867 destroyed the elegant interior. In 1864, the Victorian diarist Richard Lowry records calling in at the news room on his way home from a séance held in Nelson Street, just opposite the Arcade, off Grainger Street (see page 40).*

*The 1,000-seater concert hall in the Central Arcade c.1890. It seems strange to think that the Arcade could accommodate such opulence. T.P. Barkas, largely responsible for the expansion and success of the building at this time, was, in common with many of his contemporaries, a fervent believer in spiritualism.*

liard room, ladies' reading room, societies' reading room, lounge, tea and coffee rooms, lavatories, cloak rooms, photographic dark rooms and telephones. It also had an art gallery and 1,000-seater concert hall. There were even dressing rooms so gentlemen members could change into evening dress there if they had no time to go home before their evening engagements. The management boasted that membership offered 'more privileges than are to be had in any other club.'

On the Grey Street/Market Street sides of the building was the Central Exchange Hotel, run by John Dykes. It was well appointed with commercial rooms, billiard and smoking rooms, numerous private sitting rooms and a dining room with windows overlooking Grey Street and Market Street. Upstairs were 50 bedrooms. The hotel had a 'good class family clientèle as well as wide spread commercial connection.'

Again, fire struck the building and although the hotel survived, the news room was destroyed. No expense was spared in the redesign of the building, which re-opened in 1906 with glistening Burmantoft's ceramic tiles and a mosaic floor. The

proprietors, because by 1890, the news room had about 2,000 members. Profits were large enough to support extensive refurbishments which were completed in 1892.

The newly appointed Central Exchange News Room was a splendid and luxurious private club for ladies and gentlemen. It had a gentlemen's reading room, smoke and chess room, bil-

magnificent decoration is still preserved in the arcade today.

J.G.Windows is an old-established music shop which dominates the Grey Street side of the arcade on the site of the former hotel. Normally, it's a busy place, full of noise and music, but early in the morning or late at night, the shop takes on a very different character. Many of the staff feel that they are sharing their workplace with a person from another time.

Most of the activity takes place in the basement record department and the staff rooms which are immediately above it. This area was occupied by the lift shaft of the hotel. Sometimes staff are tapped on the shoulder or touched on the back when no customers or colleagues are nearby. One woman watched in astonishment as a CD flew out of a rack and across the room. Staff tea-breaks are sometimes disturbed by unexplained phenomena. A paper cup shot across the table, seemingly under its own power and then stopped dead. No one could have touched it. A clock flew off the wall. On one occasion, three staff members were astonished to hear a disembodied moan. The cleaner has seen a shadowy figure cross between the staff rooms and the landing. Another part of the arcade was formerly a tax office, and staff there reported seeing a young lady, dressed in servant's clothes, walking through walls.

One day, two members of Windows' staff were working in the shop outside opening hours. They sat at the top of the stairs leading to the basement to eat their sandwiches, but their meal was disturbed when they heard footsteps running down the stairs behind them. No one had passed them – there was no one else in the shop. In fact there was no one else in the entire arcade as the other shops were shut. The sound of the footsteps

*The Central Exchange Hotel, 14 August 1917. Who is the shadowy figure looking from the upper window?*

*The Central Exchange, c.1990. The upper floors, not visible from the ground, can be seen in this photograph.*

could not have emanated from another part of the building. Sometimes staff can hear people coming down a staircase that was removed in alterations to the building many years ago.

One story is that a waitress employed in the hotel realised that she was pregnant. She knew that as soon as her condition was discovered she would lose her job, and possibly the support of her family and friends too. Rather than face a miserable future, friendless and in poverty, she threw herself down the lift shaft to her death.

## THE GREY LADY OF THE ASSEMBLY ROOMS

Newcastle Assembly Rooms, on Westgate Road, was opened on 24 June 1776. The building, designed by William Newton, cost £6,700 which was financed by 129 prominent citizens, each buying a £25 share. It was intended to become the meeting place for Newcastle's high society, a venue for dazzling balls and fashionable concerts. Many of the building's original features remain today, including fine plasterwork, heavy double doors and a magnificent chandelier lighting system, made from 10,000 pieces of hand cut Newcastle Crystal.

Over the years, the Assembly Rooms has received many royal visitors: Edward VII was entertained here when he opened the Royal Victoria Infirmary and the Edward VII Bridge, George V and Queen Mary in 1928 when they opened the Tyne Bridge, and George VI and Queen Elizabeth in 1939 when they launched the battleship *KG5*. The building has also hosted a ball for the Duke of Wellington to celebrate his visit to the town in 1827, and three playlets performed by Charles Dickens and his amateur theatrical company. Musicians who have performed here include Strauss, who gave a concert on

*The Assembly Rooms, 1776.*

20 October 1838 and provided music for a ball on 19 November in the same year, Liszt, who gave a piano recital in 1841, the singer Jenny Lind, Rachmaninov and Arthur Rubinstein.

But if the legends are true, the glitter and glamour of the Old Assembly Rooms hides a tragic and shameful secret. According to one story, on 31 December 1777, some wealthy young rakes were seeing in the New Year in one of the upstairs rooms. The more they drank, the more degenerate and outrageous their behaviour became. Eventually, one young blade demanded that his wife dance naked for his friends. She did what he asked, but afterwards, overcome by shame and humiliation, she climbed the spiral staircase to the musicians' gallery and threw herself to her death on the ballroom floor below.

*The ballroom in the Assembly Rooms, photographed 6 September 1933. The musicians' gallery is at the end of the room.*

Now, staff are convinced that they share the building with the spirit of this sad lady. She always announces her presence by the scent of lavender and the rustle of a taffeta ball gown. The double doors, which are too heavy to be blown open by drafts, open and shut again as though someone has just passed through.

On Halloween 2000, the Assembly Rooms featured in a radio broadcast by Metro Radio's Alan Robson. The idea was to have live reports from a record number of haunted sites throughout Britain. Four researchers went to the Assembly Rooms and at the beginning of the broadcast, each occupied a different room on the first floor of the building. The ghost, normally benign, must have disliked publicity. There were so many unexplained noises and knockings, that by the end of the broadcast, the four terrified researchers were huddled together in one room, afraid to move around the building.

## The Pink Lady of La Sagesse

La Sagesse Convent in Jesmond is a long-established school for girls. It also has a long-established ghost, The Pink Lady. She has appeared in various classrooms, corridors and cloak-rooms, particularly to the younger girls. The place most associated with the Pink Lady, however, is a dark, narrow little stair, leading to an attic bedroom and then to the roof.

The Victorian gothic building housing La Sagesse is Jesmond Towers, once the home of Walker shipping magnate, Charles Mitchell. Mitchell bought the house in 1869 and spent a great deal of money enlarging and improving it. When he found that his land was divided by a right of way, he had a tunnel built under his drive so the public could walk underneath without disturbing the privacy of the Mitchell family. Mitchell's great passion was art – his son, Charles William Mitchell, was a respected artist – and he had an extensive and valuable art collection. In 1885 work was completed on a purpose built picture gallery attached to the towers. In an insurance inventory from 1883, the house itself was valued at £14,000, pictures £8127, sculpture £3335, jewellry etc., £2085.

By contrast the valuation for all the servants' effects in the house was just £150.

In the midst of this opulent lifestyle, tragedy struck the Mitchell family. In April 1890, Mitchell's widowed sister-in-law, Emily Cooke, came to stay at Jesmond Towers. According to reports, she had been in delicate health and showed symptoms of despondency. On the morning of May 2, Mitchell met Emily at breakfast, then went to work in his study. Within a few minutes he was disturbed by a thud on the concrete outside. Emily was lying on the ground. Mitchell and various servants rushed to her aid, but she was probably dead before they reached her. The door to the roof was open and there were footprints on the wet lead. After breakfast, Emily had climbed the dark, narrow little stair, and thrown herself to her death on the concrete, 54 feet below.

Perhaps it is Emily's ghost which returns as the Pink Lady. Girls who have attended the school in more recent years sometimes talk of a white lady. It has been recorded that ghosts sometimes fade over time, from a red lady, losing colour as the years go by, first to pink, then to white.

*Jesmond Towers c.1920.*

# Purveyors of Ales, Wines … and Spirits?

## The Blackie Boy

The Blackie Boy (also known as the Black Boy Inn) in the Groat Market is one of the oldest pubs in Newcastle. When it was sold in 1829, an advertisement described its stabling, malt kiln, brewing apparatus, a pump of excellent water in the yard and a long room in which 200 people could eat. The inn was rebuilt at the end of the 19th century when part of the structure collapsed.

In the evenings, especially at weekends, it is usually crowded with drinkers enjoying the lively atmosphere of the Bigg Market area. At other times, however, particularly after hours, it can be quite eerie. Several staff have reported feeling a presence or hearing unexplained thuds. Two of the most astonishing occurrences have happened in broad daylight.

One day a member of staff was changing a light bulb in the upstairs toilet. Suddenly a woman's voice yelled out 'What are you doing in here?' The voice came from one of the cubicles which he knew to be empty. As he hesitated, the voice screamed, 'Get out, get out, get out!' The man was so startled that he tripped on the stairs in his haste to leave. The commotion alerted his colleagues who rushed upstairs, picked him up and investigated the toilets. Of course there was no one there.

A few years earlier, when the pub was being refurbished, one of the design team sat in an upstairs room, painting some jugs. As she concentrated on her work, she felt she was being watched. The room seemed empty, but there was definitely a presence behind her, and for some reason she could tell that he was male. She could feel him breathing on her neck.

The Blackie Boy was one of the favourite establishments of the famous engraver, Thomas Bewick. He belonged to a club – known as Swarley's, after the inn's proprietor, Richard Swarley – which met there. Bewick described the other members as merchants or respectable tradesmen. He said that there were few rules except that every member should behave with decorum and as a gentleman. If anyone transgressed, he was

*The Black Boy Inn c.1965, with the Flying Horse beyond, just before Thompson House was built.*

*A very early photograph of the Groat Market, looking north, c.1854. The old houses on the right were removed when the building of the Town Hall began in 1855.*

just below Wilson's Court. For the most part it was a respectable establishment, but one room was known locally as Hell's Kitchen. Ruffians, tramps and the low life of the town came to drink here. The very names of the regulars sound like trouble: Euphy Scott, Queen of the fishwives and Owld Judy, guardian of the town hutch. Blind Willie Purvis also drank here. He composed a song called *Buy Brooms Besums*, undoubtedly popular in his day, but one which has probably not been sung in the vicinity of the Bigg Market for very many years!

The landlord, Ralph Nicholson, ruled his clients with an iron fist. He took the precaution of chaining the four foot long poker to the fireplace, just in case it occurred to anyone to use it as a weapon. If an argument broke out, Nicholson would lock the doors and stop anyone leaving until calm was restored. Any serious breach of Hell's Kitchen etiquette was punished by a six months ban. Only after the offender had given a personal guarantee of good behaviour, would Nicholson readmit him or her.

Perhaps the spirit of one of the Hell's Kitchen regulars was disturbed when her old haunt was demolished. As a life long drinker, there would be no attraction in spending eternity in a newspaper office, so perhaps she moved to the nearest surviving pub, the Blackie Boy.

immediately fined. If he did not pay, he was 'sent to Coventry' or dismissed from the club.

Perhaps the quiet gentleman who took such an interest in the designer's work was a member of this very proper society. But the genteel Swarley's club would never have admitted a woman, much less a harpy like the one who screamed from the toilet cubicle. However, rough, low class women did frequent a nearby inn known as the Flying Horse.

The Flying Horse stood on the site of Thompson House,

## THE FRUSTRATED TRAVELLER

The former Jesmond Station is a grade two listed building dating from 1864. In 1981 it was converted into a pub called The Carriage. The present manageress took over the pub 13 years ago, and since then, she and her family and staff have realised that they share the building with another being who is looking for attention.

One evening the manageress had locked up after closing time and was sitting talking to the last remaining member of staff as they waited for a taxi. Suddenly, the manageress realised that someone was standing behind her. Without thinking, she moved her stool to allow them to pass. It was only when a grey shape slid past her and disappeared that she realised that the only other person in the building was sitting right in front of her, still talking to her. Other staff often feel that there is someone standing behind them, waiting to pass. They always move out of the way, only to realise that there is no one there. One of the cleaners has become so used to this presence that she calls him George.

The manageress's son, on the other hand, sees a female figure in the grey shadow. He has had a more alarming experience with the phantom. While he was helping his mother wash up in the kitchen, a fish slice and ladle, which had been hanging on the window grille, flew off and hit him on the chest. It isn't the only time the phantom has resorted to throwing things in an effort to be noticed. Coins lined around the bar for a charity collection shot to the floor as though they had been pushed. Glasses fall off shelves, but always land the right way up without breaking. On one occasion the cook had

gone into the cellar and felt that someone was there with her. She guessed that the boss had sneaked in to frighten her, and decided to turn the tables on him by hiding and jumping out. Eventually she realised that she was, after all, alone in the cellar but as she emerged from her hiding place a glass flew off a ledge and smashed against a sink on the wall opposite.

No one is certain who the phantom is, but according to local tradition, an exploding bomb killed two passengers standing on the station platform during World War II. However, although parts of Jesmond were damaged by bombs, there is no record of one falling near enough to the station to kill passengers.

*Jesmond Station in 1977, before it was converted to a pub.*

# SHADES IN SHOPS

*Robinson's Booksellers in the Grainger Market is very little changed from how it must have looked over 100 years ago. Recent disturbances in the bookshop may have been the work of spirits from long ago as the markets, designed by John Dobson, were opened on 24 October 1835.*

## THE TALE OF A BOOKWORM

One of the best known stalls in the Grainger Market is Robinson's bookshop. Founded in 1881, the shop moved to its present site a few years later. Today the shop looks very much the same as it did 120 years ago.

It's a good place for book lovers to browse and pick up bargains, but for a few weeks in the summer of 2000, one mysterious bibliophile made visits to the shop at night. Each evening, the owner locked the shop, leaving everything in its proper place. When he returned in the morning to open up, he'd find that the stock had been moved around. Some books were lying open, as though someone had been reading them. The disturbances continued for a few weeks, and then ceased, as abruptly as they had started.

No one knows what caused the disturbances, or why they only lasted a short time. There is possible connection with another bookseller called Robinson who opened a shop at the corner of Shakespeare Street in 1840. This man, Robert Robinson, is thought to be related to the Robinsons of Grainger Market. He published Bewick's *Life and Times* and his shop was known as Bewick's Head. He loved books so much that he often slept in the shop so he could be near his treasures. Perhaps his spirit wandered into the shop that bears his family name so he could spend a few more nights in the company of books.

## THE SMILING NUN

Opposite the fire station, at 38-40 Pilgrim Street, is a shop which is now a fashion shop called Leaf. It's a grade two listed building and dates from around 1837. For many years it was Scott's umbrella shop and factory.

In 1970, a woman customer on the first floor of the shop

*Pilgrim Street, c.1945.*

always felt a drop in temperature before she appeared.

The building stands on land once owned by the friary of the Grey Friars. But if the ghostly nun has returned from this period of the city's history, how did she acquire horn-rimmed glasses? Perhaps the mystery will never be explained. The owners of Leaf opened their shop 24 years ago and have not seen her in all that time.

## CELLAR 9

The North Eastern Co-op on Newgate Street is a splendid Art Deco building, designed in 1929. It was intended to be the flagship store for a huge organisation which had grown from very humble beginnings,

*The Co-op, Newgate Street, 1946.*

saw the figure of a nun, wearing horn-rimmed glasses. The nun, who seemed to be perfectly solid and substantial, looked at the woman and smiled. The customer realised there was something out of place and mentioned it to the shop's owner. He said that the nun was the shop's own ghost. Several other people had seen her, particularly the shop's bookkeeper who

nearly 70 years earlier.

The first Co-op in Newcastle opened on February 18, 1861, in a tiny shop on Nelson Street. The entire stock of flour and groceries was worth £17 7s 7½d (£17.38). The 11 founder members were all employed elsewhere, so the shop could open

*A hidden side of Black Friars, to the rear of the Co-op, photographed in 1965. Perhaps the Co-op ghost came from these old monastic buildings.*

*Darn Crook in 1899, before the Co-op was built. Possibly the ghost has a connection with these old buildings, or with St Andrew's churchyard on the right.*

The splendid new store had some of the most stylish and modern design features of the day, including wavy ballustrades and Egyptian style pillars. But behind the grand facade some features of the older Co-op building remain. Below street-level is a warren of cellars used as store rooms. They are very cold, and in bad weather prone to flooding. One particular cellar, cellar nine, was used to store soap. It was also said to be haunted by the ghost of a monk from nearby Black Friars Friary. Many of the staff, including hard-headed, down-to-earth men, had an aversion to entering this cellar alone. A former worker remembers that some parts of the cellar were colder and more shadowy than others, and often felt that a presence was standing or moving close to her when in fact there was nothing and no one there.

The same staff member worked in the Co-op pharmacy office and shared a room with two colleagues on the second floor, overlooking Darn Crook. The office was quite isolated from the rest of the building as it was at the top of a flight of wooden stairs. Other workers would have had very little reason to pass the door. Often, however, there would be a distinct knock at the door. When it was opened, there was no one there, and no sign of giggling colleagues rushing down the stairs. One of the younger warehousemen saw a burly man, dressed in some sort of dark coat, climbing the same flight of stairs. He disappeared before he reached the top.

only in the evenings after they had finished work. By the end of the first trading year, however, the shop was successful enough to justify a full time sales assistant who was paid 24s (£1.20) each week. The Co-op went from strength to strength, and soon there were branches all over the city centre and suburbs.

By 1929, the organisation was so successful that plans were made to demolish part of the existing store on Newgate Street, and replace it with the magnificent building which still stands today. The first phase, a completely new frontage, was completed in 1932 and other building work, mostly on the interior, was completed in the following year.

# TWO CHILDREN

## THE BOY IN THE BASEMENT

The building which stands on the corner of Grainger Street and the Bigg Market is, at the time of writing, a branch of Pizza Hut. It is haunted by the ghost of a small boy, dressed in Victorian clothing, complete with beribboned hat. From time to time he appears in the basement, stands quietly beside the dishwasher for a minute or two, and then vanishes.

In the later years of the 19th century the building was occupied first by a hatter called J. Campbell, and then by a branch of Manfield & Sons, boot and shoe makers. By 1895 Manfield had a factory in Northampton and branches in London, Liverpool, Glasgow, Manchester, Birmingham, Leeds, Bradford, Hull, Nottingham, Newcastle and, surprisingly, Paris. In fact the company was awarded the gold medal for excellence in the manufacture of boots at the Paris Exhibition of 1889. The lowest priced boots in the shop cost 10s 6d (52.5p) – the price was displayed prominently in the window – but wealthier clients could buy hand sewn moor and shooting boots at 45s (£2.25) as well as 'the latest and most fashionable styles in ladies and gents walking shoes and general boots and shoes.'

*Manfield and Sons c.1894, on the corner of Grainger Street and the Bigg Market.*

At this time in the building's history, the first floor was occupied by a restaurant, and the second floor by dwellings. But there's no clue to the identity of the small Victorian boy who stands so quietly in the basement.

*Eldon Square, built by Richard Grainger in 1825-31, photographed on 26 January 1914 when it was being altered as part of an improvement scheme. The ornamental shrubbery has been removed. A little girl seems to haunt the attic of No. 7 Eldon Square, the last house on the right hand stretch of houses. The arch beyond was for coaches to reach the rear of the properties. The whole of the back range was demolished to make way for the Eldon Square Shopping Centre.*

## THE GIRL IN THE ATTIC

Old Eldon Square was built by Richard Grainger between 1825 and 1831. It featured Palladian houses, built round an ornamental shrubbery, and was immediately acknowledged as the town's most graceful development. Gentlemen and professional men, such as doctors and solicitors, made their homes here. During the 1840s and 50s, No. 7 was the home of Edward Charlton, MD. Much of the square was demolished during the development of the Eldon Square Mall in the 1970s, and most of the remaining nineteenth century buildings are now shops.

Recently a young girl did work experience in the shop at 7 Old Eldon Square. Part of her job was to fetch stock from the attic storeroom.

Sometimes, when she unlocked the room, she could hear the sound of a little girl's voice chucking and laughing softly. She also heard a strange, metallic, rolling noise. When she later visited Beamish Museum and heard the sound of metal hoops being bowled in the school yard, she immediately connected it with the noise she had heard in the attic.

The girl never saw anything to accompany the sounds in the attic, and when she asked her colleagues, none of them had experienced anything out of the ordinary there. She had a strong feeling that the little spirit was identifying with her because of her age and that the invisible child simply wanted another young person to play with. Sometimes, she even thought she heard sobs as she finished her work in the attic and locked the door, leaving the ghostly little girl all alone.

*A boy stands at the south-west corner of the Eldon Square gardens, before they were removed, in 1914.*

# Weird happenings at work

### The jingling ghost

New England House on Ridley Place is a modern office building standing on the site of the old Central Methodist church. The church, opened in October 1899, fronted onto Northumberland Road with the Sunday School on Ridley Place. The building, which cost over £15,000, was rather grand and featured a Gothic front with a spire. In 1978, with the congregation dwindling, it was decided to close the church and the site was redeveloped as New England House.

For 13 years during the 1980s and 1990s, the first floor of New England House was occupied by a financial services company … and something – or someone – else.

During the time the company was based there, every member of staff seemed to have something to report. Workers arriving in the morning felt that there was already someone in the building as they entered. The workspace consisted of a long office with three small interview rooms at one end. The rooms were divided from the main office by frosted glass windows. Often workers could see shapes moving behind the frosted glass when they knew the rooms were empty.

One young man used to jingle the change in his pocket as he walked. Colleagues could hear him coming before they saw him. One day, some members of staff were sitting with their backs to the door of the main office. They heard a jingling sound and guessed that their colleague had come into the room, playing with his change as usual. They turned round to greet him, but there was no one there.

The same young man was working overtime one evening. He was sitting in one of the interview rooms, concentrating on

*The Central Methodist Church on Northumberland Road, c.1900.*

*Ridley Place, 1966. The rear Sunday School of the Central Methodist Church is half-way down on the right. The site is now occupied by a modern office building, but staff have sensed the presence of something strange on the first floor, at the level at which the church's balcony had been.*

his work, when he heard someone come into the main office. Nobody else should have been around at that time of night, so he went out to investigate. There was no one there. He was so unnerved by the experience that he decided to go home and finish his work another day. The boss had similar experiences when he came into work at weekends. The office was quiet, and he distinctly heard someone coming into the building through the front door. When he went to check, there was never anyone there.

One night the cleaners had finished all their work. They were convinced that the building was empty, all the internal doors were locked and all the lights extinguished. As they stood in the street, locking the main door, they noticed that the first floor lights were blazing. But they had clear recollections of putting them out. Wearily, they returned to the building to extinguish the lights and check that the offices were indeed empty. There was no one at all in the building, but they all sensed a definite presence.

One of the cleaners often used to see an apparition in the first floor offices. She described it as a shadow, like a man wearing a long coat. She felt quite comfortable with him, and worked around him as though he wasn't there.

Puzzled by these strange experiences, one member of staff decided to do some investigating and see what she could find out about the building. She located some people who used to belong to the congregation of the Methodist church which used to stand on the site of the office block. They remembered similar strange happenings, usually connected with the church's balcony. The balcony was on the same level as the first floor offices where all the activity was concentrated. Was the shadowy figure in the long coat a member of the chapel's original congregation, or perhaps the spirit of a minister wearing clerical dress?

## THE GHOST WHICH WALKED THROUGH LOCKED DOORS

Hawthorn Leslie, one of Newcastle's most famous engineering companies, operated from a sprawling complex of buildings on Forth Banks which rises steeply from the quayside to the back of the Central Station. Some years ago, one of the old Hawthorn Leslie buildings, at that time called Forth Banks House, was used as premises for Dial-a-Ride, an employment training scheme.

Because it is built on such a steep hill, it is a strange split-level building. Underground are vast cellars, parts of which are mysteriously blocked off. The long corridors in the building have been divided by doors at regular intervals. Each section of corridor had a separate alarm.

People in Forth Banks House realised that there was a problem when, night after night, the alarms were activated. It

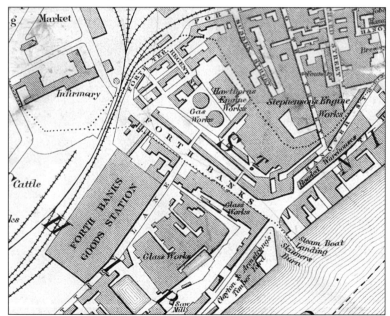

*Forth Banks, 1878. Hawthorn Leslie's engineering works expanded to fill much of the area to the east of Forth Banks.*

usually happened between one and two o' clock in the morning. There was never any sign of a break in. Each time the alarm went off, a service engineer would be called out to check the system. Nobody was ever able to identify a fault.

Understandably, the management became perturbed at the huge amount of money they were paying in call-out charges. Eventually the main keyholder decided that he and an engineer would spend the night in the building to discover what was actually happening.

*Cows from the nearby cattle market on Forth Banks, on their way to the Quayside, c.1900.*

Shortly after one o' clock, one of the corridor alarms went off, rapidly followed by another and another. The two men were amazed. It seemed as though something was moving along the corridor, up the stairs and onto the next floor. Yet, apart from themselves, the building was empty. They wondered if an animal was activating the alarms. It was impossible. The doors dividing the corridors remained firmly locked. Whatever was moving through the building was passing through solid doors. The two men wrote in the log book for that night 'Alarms activated by ghost'!

# SECRETS OF THE CASTLE GARTH

**A FRONTIER STRONGHOLD**

Newcastle takes its name from the 'New Castle', founded in 1080 by Robert Curthose, eldest son of William the Conqueror. Built on top of the possible site of a Roman fort at Pons Aelius, and an Anglo-Saxon cemetery, the early castle was a fortified enclosure surrounded by a clay rampart, probably topped by a timber palisade, and a clay ditch.

Between 1168 and 1178, the Castle was rebuilt in stone at a cost of £1,144 5s 6d. Over the years it was enlarged, altered and improved. Not all of the alterations were completed. On the second floor, a 15 step staircase ends abruptly in solid masonry. It is thought that an invasion of William the Lion of Scotland in 1174 ended the rebuilding programme.

The last part of the defences, the Black Gate, was added between 1247 and 1250. It is called the Black Gate, not to strike terror into the hearts of the invading enemy, but after Patrick Black, a London merchant, who leased the gatehouse in the 17th century and lived there with his wife Barbara.

Originally, the castle was a real frontier stronghold; a vital part of England's defence against the Scots, and it is a magnificent example of medieval engineering. Offset windows and doors meant that a chance arrow, fired in through one of the narrow windows, could travel only a very short distance before hitting a wall, thus greatly decreasing the risk of it wounding or killing anyone. The water supply, from the Keep's 100-foot-deep well, comes into the building on the second floor. From the well room, a system of sinks and lead pipes meant that water could be distributed to lower parts of the Keep, including the ground floor garrison room. If the lower floors were occupied by the enemy, the defenders on the upper floor would still have water, but they could cut off the attackers' supply. The system also prevented an invading army from poisoning the Castle's water. Even the latrines are designed so that nobody could climb the waste channel and

*The Castle Keep and surrounding buildings in 1789, before the restorers got their hands on it.*

gain entrance to the Keep without being spotted.

In 1305, the Scots warrior William Wallace was hanged, drawn and quartered in London. It was a horrifyingly brutal death, but not his final humiliation. To display the might of the Crown, and to discourage other attacks on English authority, Wallace's body parts were distributed around England and Scotland. His head was placed on London Bridge, his right leg went to Perth, his left to Aberdeen. His left arm went to Berwick. His right arm was exhibited on the bridge at Newcastle, while other, unnamed body parts made a gruesome display on Newcastle Keep.

Newcastle's town walls were completed around the middle of the 14th century, and with the changing political situation, the strategic importance of the Castle declined. By 1589 it was described as old and ruinous. In the 17th century, houses were built in the defended passageway behind the Black Gate, and the Black Gate itself had become a public house, run by John Pickells, whose name and the date 1636 can be seen high on the south-west wall.

Just a few years later, Pickells and his neighbours probably had cause to regret living so close to the Castle, when it saw action once again during the Civil War. In the room known as the King's chamber, the names of two Cromwellian prisoners held in the Castle have left their names, John Danby and Thomas Cuthbert, carved into the stone, along with a date – 10/1644, the date of the siege of Newcastle.

Newcastle has the distinction of using human ordure in the defence of the town against the enemy. By the time of the civil war, a dung heap, 98 yards long, 10 yards high and 32 yards wide, had accumulated near the Castle. Sir John Marley used the dung to ramier or support the town walls during the siege.

## THE BLOODSTAINED CHAMBER

On the north side of the Great Hall, a small flight of stairs leads up to a window. A smaller set of stairs goes off to the left to a small room with its own latrine and a tiny slit window. In the walls of the short passage leading to this room, there are holes for three sets of hinges, suggesting that this room was once separated from the body of the Keep by three doors. Obviously something, or someone, very important was kept here.

It has been suggested that this room was once the powder store of the Castle. But why build a latrine in a room not intended for human occupation? Holes in the stonework indicate that a thick draw bar would have been placed in front of the innermost door, providing additional security. This would have been useless in keeping people out of the room, but very effective in keeping someone inside. It seems likely that the room was not a store, but a

*The guardroom on the lower floor of the Castle c.1810. The pillar with its iron rings for chains is still there.*

*A door in the Castle around 1810.*

prison cell.

In the corner of the room, opposite the door and beside the window, there are mysterious red stains in the sandstone at about head height. The stains could be traces of iron in the stone, but this seems unlikely. They are concentrated in one small area, the stains run through the mortar as well as the stone and they have hard edges. It looks as though red liquid has been spattered across the wall. Was the liquid blood? In the atmosphere of this frontier stronghold it is a tempting conclusion. Perhaps a prisoner met a violent end while attempting to escape from his dark little cell. Perhaps it was too troublesome to keep someone confined there, so his guards arranged a bloody 'accident'. Nothing so far found in the records of the Castle explains the stains.

## THE FLYING DONKEY

On 7 December, 1733, a showman advertised that he would fly from the top of the Castle Keep. This sort of thing didn't happen in Newcastle every day, so a huge crowd gathered to see the spectacle. At the top of the 100-foot-high tower, the showman was becoming rather anxious. It was an awfully long way down, and his strap-on wings hadn't had much of a test flight. In the interests of scientific research, he decided to send his donkey down first. Donkeys are not exactly aerodynamic, and the poor beast didn't even know how to flap his wings, so he dropped like a stone. Amazingly, the animal survived his flight. It probably helped that his fall was broken by a spectator who died as a result. The commotion caused by this most unusual accident meant that the showman was not obliged to fulfil his boast and make the flight.

## TRAGEDY AT HIGH NOON

By the end of the 18th century, the Castle was in a state of extreme disrepair and bore very little resemblance to a defensive structure. Mr Ffyfes, landlord of the Three Bulls' Heads, was using the chapel as a beer cellar, a confectioner had dug an icehouse out of the wall in the south-west corner of the Keep, and the roof of the Keep was being used as a cabbage garden. A warren of houses had sprung up around Castle Garth. Some of the dwellings were four storeys high, but only ten feet wide. The Black Gate had become a slum tenement, housing anything up to 60 people, and at one time it was even used as a brothel.

In 1810, Newcastle Corporation bought the remains of the Castle, including the Keep, for 600 guineas. Over the next three years the building was restored. As a reminder of its for-

*The Black Gate in a dilapidated state around 1860.*

*The restored roof of the Keep in 1913. The gun may or may not be the one that fired the fatal shot.*

hot enough to light the second charge before Robson was ready. The explosion blew off Robson's right hand and threw his body to the foot of the Keep.

Firing the noonday gun was soon discontinued – not because of Robson's death, but because of the damage it was causing to the buildings surrounding the Keep. When the gun was fired, burning wadding would fly out of the bore, often setting fire to the wooden roofs of the densely packed houses in Castle Garth.

## THE SHRINKING STAIRS

Despite the Castle's bloody past, workers are unaware of specific hauntings. However, when the custodian locks the main door last thing at night, and comes down the stone staircase to pavement level, he sometimes has a strange experience. He has a compelling feeling that the staircase has ended too soon, and that there ought to be a few more steps down.

He is absolutely right. The present pavement level was created by the Victorians during their restoration, and the original staircase would indeed have continued further.

mer glory, the authorities decided to fire a cannon from the roof of the Keep at noon each day, and on special occasions. This ceremony was to have tragic consequences.

At noon on 7 May, 1812, Gunner John Robson fired the first shot from the roof of the Keep. He started to load the cannon for the second shot, but forgot to swab out the cannon first. There was still burning powder inside the bore. It was

# RAISING THE DEAD

In 1864, a number of Newcastle's most prominent citizens gathered in a small room to witness some very strange occurrences. They were following a craze that was sweeping Europe and America – spiritualism. And their guides were the Davenport brothers, two of the most celebrated mediums of the day.

Ira and William Davenport were born in Buffalo, New York. As children they began to experiment with spiritualism. Soon reports circulated that the boys were at the centre of some astonishing phenomena. Violins were said to float round the room, playing themselves. The teenagers were lifted towards the ceiling by some unseen agency.

As the Davenports' fame spread they became celebrities, touring at home in the USA and abroad, demonstrating their spectacular powers. They arrived in Newcastle in 1864 and gave two séances in Baker's Temperance Hotel, Westgate Street.

They were accompanied by W.F. Fay, a 25-year-old American who had been a practising medium for 11 years. He claimed that he first recognised his powers when he was play-ing marbles with friends and an invisible force lifted him into the air and set him down in the branches of a tree. Unfortun-ately, the reaction of his friends to this alarming incident is not recorded. Dr J.B. Ferguson, the fourth member of the party, acted as master of ceremonies.

Twenty-six local worthies assembled to see the spectacle. They included Joseph Cowen, Newcastle's MP from 1865 to 1873, John Mawson, chemist and druggist, who was to become Sheriff of Newcastle in 1867, and T.P. Barkas, later proprietor of the Central Exchange News Room. Barkas was a fervent believer in spiritualism, and published several pamphlets on the subject. The following description is based on his record of the séance.

The gentlemen gathered in a darkened room, lit only by a

*T.P. Barkas, 1874, from a portrait in* **The Newcastle Critic.**

chandelier. The focal point of the first part of the séance was the cabinet which always accompanied the Davenports on tour. The audience was invited to examine it minutely. It stood on trestles and was tall enough to allow a man to stand upright inside. The floor was carpeted and seats were fixed against the walls. The front of the cabinet was closed by three doors. The central door featured a lozenge shaped hole, covered by a curtain.

Two volunteers from the audience bound the Davenports to the seats inside the cabinet using ordinary clothes line. When they were satisfied that the brothers could not move, they placed a variety of musical instruments including guitars, a tambourine, a trumpet and a violin around the interior of the cabinet. Dr Ferguson closed the doors and bolted two of them, explaining that the third would be locked from the inside by a mysterious force.

The lights were lowered and, as promised, the audience heard the sound of the third door locking. Then the trumpet was thrown through the hole in the door. The cabinet was opened to reveal that the Davenports were still securely tied in their original positions. Once more the doors were closed, and this time the audience was treated to a musical interlude as the guitar was strummed and the tambourine jingled before the trumpet was one again thrown out of the hole.

Again the doors were opened and again the Davenports remained tied in position. This time it was suggested that one of the audience might like to share their captivity. The man chosen was a clergyman, the Rev. Mr Taylor. He sat between the brothers with one hand touching each man to ensure they did not move. The doors closed and the brave minister was left to his fate. Again came the sound of the musical instruments. When the doors were opened, Rev. Taylor was found with the tambourine placed firmly on his head. Not in the least disconcerted by this undignified headgear, he affirmed

that the brothers had not moved during the whole performance, but that he had felt a hand, like a human hand but cold and damp, touching him on the face and beard.

Finally, the doors were closed again and the audience could hear the sounds of ropes being untied. In a few seconds the doors flew open and the brothers stepped out completely free. There was not the slightest indication, in the form of flushed faces or rapid pulses, that they had undergone any physical exertion.

For the second part of the séance, a table was brought into the room and two guitars and a tambourine were placed upon it. Mr Fay and Ira Davenport were tied to chairs. William Davenport and Dr Ferguson each sat between two members of the audience who held their hands to ensure they did not move. Finally, the rest of the audience was asked to join hands and to remain that way until the end of the séance, and bound on their honour not to strike any light while the proceedings were underway.

The lights were extinguished and the room was in total darkness. Instantly, the sounds of the musical instruments were heard. To relieve the repetitiveness of this spiritual concert, some miserable members of the audience felt sharp blows to their heads and bodies as the instruments moved swiftly and erratically round the room.

Then Mr Ward, a member of the audience, broke his word and stuck a match. The manifestations instantly ceased. Dr Ferguson was furious and declared that the séance would not continue until Mr Ward had left the room. Mr Ward retorted that he was trying to detect a swindle and in fact his match had revealed William Davenport standing in the middle of the room. Mr Stephenson and John Mawson, the two men who had been holding Davenport declared that he did not leave his seat until after the match had been struck.

Mr Ward gave his word that he would cause no further

*The Victorians, rich and poor, were fascinated by spiritualism and séances, as evidenced by the sell-out performances of the Davenports, and the prices that people were prepared to pay. There certainly seems to have been a willing suspension of disbelief. A crowded Grainger Street, c.1890.*

*From the **Newcastle Courant**, Friday 21 October, 1864.*

disturbance and the manifestations continued in a similar vein.

The evening séance was tediously similar to the first, except that in the darkness, Mr Fay's coat was removed without disturbing his bindings. Mr Reed, a member of the audience, asked if his own coat could be put on Mr Fay in a similar fashion. Sure enough, the lights were turned off, a rushing sound was heard, and when they were turned on again, Mr Fay was wearing Mr Reed's coat although the ropes that tied him were still in place.

Despite Mr Ward's accusations, everyone else present at both séances seemed to accept without question that all the phenomena were genuine and that there was no trickery involved. But if spirits really had visited Baker's Temperance Hotel on Westgate Street, surely they could have produced something more challenging than the monotonous strummings of instruments and the slapstick indignities inflicted on members of the audience.

Everything that happened inside the cabinet could have been the work of an accomplice, concealed, perhaps beneath a false floor. Alternatively, the Davenports could have had the ability to escape from the ropes, then return to them at high speed. The great escapologist, Houdini, made a name and a fortune from feats like this. Rev. Mr Taylor would have been too concerned with holding tightly to the Davenports and too alarmed about what he might encounter shut up there in the darkness, to think too closely about what was producing the sounds and sensations. He admitted that the hand that touched him felt like a human hand, but he did not draw the most obvious conclusion that it *was* a human hand attached to a living human body.

Mr Ward said that he had seen William Davenport standing in the centre of the room when he was supposed to have been sitting, firmly held by Messrs Mawson and Stephenson, but his evidence was conveniently ignored. Those gentlemen swore that Davenport had not moved, but they could have been duped. It was not unusual that members of an audience who thought they were holding tightly to a medium were in fact clinging to each other while the medium was elsewhere giving the phenomena a helping hand.

A remarkably similar 'exposure' occurred in Cheltenham, probably during the same tour. John Nevil Maskelyne, later to become a conjuror, was a watchmaker in the town. One day, an American came into his shop, asking him to repair a strange piece of equipment. Maskelyne asked what the machine was, but the American was evasive. When the repair was complete, the American gave Maskelyne a large tip saying, 'I'm sure a smart young fellow like you could use the loose change. And in return, just forget you ever saw me.'

Later, Maskelyne saw posters for the Davenports' séance in Cheltenham and he recognised one of the men on the poster as the American who had come into his shop. It was Ira Davenport. Full of curiosity he attended the performance. He claimed later that he had disturbed the window blind and in the beam of light that entered the room the whole audience could see that both Davenports were out of their seats. However, no one in the audience came forward to corroborate his claim.

*An 1855 advertisement for the Queen's Head Inn which stretched between Pilgrim Street and Grey Street. The old house, dating from the mid-17th century on Pilgrim Street has now been restored. No manifestations have been reported.*

Maskelyne decided to copy, from memory, the machine Davenport had brought for repair. He discovered it was a device which would produce many of the phenomena in the Davenports' séances and he used it to great effect in his conjuring acts. Of course, he was as keen to preserve his trade secrets as the Davenports before him, so we still don't know what the mysterious mechanism was.

In the 19th and early 20th centuries, numerous mediums were caught in the act of committing fraud – using pulleys and concealed wires to move objects; making sighs and ethereal sounds with bellows held between the knees; walking around the audience in the guise of spirits, touching and talking to people who were convinced that the medium was at that very moment locked in her cabinet in the deepest of trances. Despite regular demonstrations that many 'psychic' phenomena owed more to engineering and conjuring than the supernatural, people were desperate to believe. In the days before modern medicine, the infant mortality rate was frighteningly high, and many couples lost one or more children. The death of a spouse at an early age was all too common. People needed to feel that these loved ones were not gone forever and the mediums gave them hope that communication did not cease after death. Consequently, they continued to be convinced by the least convincing of evidence.

*Paraffin moulds of feet of supposedly materialised spirit forms, from an account of a séance.*

The part of the Davenports' performance which it is most difficult to explain is the changing of Mr Fay's coat without disturbing his bonds. The event occurred in total darkness, so no one could see how it was done, but in many respects it sounds similar to some of the feats performed by Houdini. Harry Houdini was keen to believe in spiritualism, but was equally keen not to be duped. He decided to test mediums by attempting to replicate the phenomena they produced using, not spiritual intervention, but his skills as an escapologist. Although he tried for many, many years, he never found an effect which he could not copy. In 1910 Houdini made friends with Ira Davenport. According to some commentators, Ira, who died the next year, confessed his secrets to Houdini. Houdini never made this knowledge public, but in 1920 he wrote to his great friend Sir Arthur Conan Doyle, author of Sherlock Holmes:

*I can make a positive assertion that the Davenport Brothers never were exposed ... I know for a positive fact that it was not essential for them to release these bonds in order to obtain manifestations.*

However the Davenports produced their manifestations, the public wanted to see them. They held further séances in

Newcastle. On November 4, 1864, they performed in the long room of the Queen's Head on Pilgrim Street. This inn, now known as Alderman Fenwick's House, had been at the centre of a bodysnatching scandal in 1829. Surely if the Davenports truly had been raising displaced spirits, they should have found them at the Queen's Head. Instead the 25-strong audience, who were rich enough and interested enough to pay the considerable sum of one guinea for their tickets, were treated to the familiar routine of strumming instruments and flying trumpets. The next evening, there was a slightly less select gathering in the lecture room on Nelson Street. Tickets, costing 10s 6d (52.5p) or 5s (25p) were strictly limited to 300. This time the audience was more sceptical.

Richard Lowry of Newcastle recounts his visit to the the public lecture on 5 November in his diary:

*Went to see the Brothers Davenport in the lecture room at 7pm. About 200 highly respectable people were present – the greatest portion having preferred the 5/- to the 10/6 tickets – I got an excellent seat directly in front of the stage on which stood the cabinets in which the mysteries had to be performed. I was determined to pay the greatest attention to what I saw and heard as it was my first visit to a similar exhibition ... the audience were much disappointed ... and deemed the whole thing as a 'swindle'. In fact I was regularly disappointed myself ... neither spiritualist or animal magnetism had anything whatever to do with them ... they had done all they were in the habit of doing before a public audience and other manifestations were only done before a select audience – that is where they are paid 21/- instead of 5/-. Called in at the News Room on the way home ...*

From these lucrative beginnings, spiritualism gathered momentum throughout the 19th century. Mediums vied with each other to produce ever more spectacular effects. Ectoplasm, believed by many at the time to be the stuff of which spirits were made, issued mysteriously from the bodies of entranced mediums, and formed itself into the shapes of loved ones who had died. Photographs of the effects were produced to record the phenomena for posterity. However ectoplasm viewed with modern eyes looks surprisingly like cheesecloth.

As the popularity of spiritualism spread, some Newcastle townsfolk formed The Newcastle Society for the Investigation of Spiritualism, which had its first meeting in 1872. Over the next few months, several of the members discovered they had mediumistic powers. By 1873, two teenaged girls, Miss Wood, aged 18 and Miss Fairlamb, aged 17, had emerged as the most gifted mediums in the society.

Miss C.E. Wood was born in October, 1854, the second daughter of Thomas Wood, a mechanic from Newcastle. Her father was interested in spiritualism, and had taken her along to the Society. It is tempting to speculate that Mr Wood's mechanical expertise played no small part in his daughter's séances. When her gifts were discovered, Miss Wood was employed by the Society which spent many months investigating her powers. As her fame spread, she was invited to give séances to other spiritualist societies around the country. Some of Miss Wood's manifestations bore striking similarities to those produced by the Davenports. On one occasion, her hands and elbows were tied to her chair, the lights were extinguished and when they were relit, an iron ring, which had been on the table, was found to be on her right arm, although the bindings still appeared to be secure. Sometimes, spectators found that in the darkness, their hats, bonnets and slippers had been exchanged for those of other members of the group, some of the sitters were hit with a paper tube, and notes would sound on the piano. But Miss Wood was also able to produce more spectacular effects, often when she was tied to a chair, in full view of the audience. Our old friend T.P. Barkas reports:

*A facsimile supposedly from a photograph showing a mark in the film made by the spirit 'Pocka', while the film was in the camera.*

*I have seen through the mediumship of Miss Wood ... living forms walk from the curtained recess, which it was utterly impossible for her to simulate. I have seen children, women and men of various ages, walk forth under her mediumship. I have seen a materialised form and the medium at the same time. I have had through her mediumship a childlike form standing beside me for about half an hour together; the child has placed its arms around my neck, and permitted me at the same time to place my arm around her neck, and has laid its cheek against mine, breathed upon my face ... This was not in darkness, but in light, and in the presence of professors and fellows of one of the leading universities in the kingdom.*

At one séance, held at Portobello, near Chester-le-Street, a spirit form appeared, which one of the sitters recognised as his dead wife. He spoke to her, and other members of the group shook hands with her. Other spirits graced other meetings, including a burly Scots spirit called Benny and a gentle feminine creature called Meggie. It's interesting to note how often spectators stressed that these spirits were exactly like human

*Portraits, like this one, of dead children, were not seen as macabre or morbid. When childhood mortality was frighteningly high, the miraculous new technique of photography could provide grieving parents with a lasting reminder of their loved one.*

beings. When Benny was asked to eat an apple, the audience could hear him bite; when he was asked to dance, the room shook. He cut off a portion of his beard and gave it to a member of the audience who kept it as a souvenir. Yet believers were adamant that these very real people were not accomplices of the medium. Because the audience members thought they had taken all necessary precautions to exclude accomplices from the séance, they would not admit to the possibility of trickery. The fact that Benny was so large and Meggie so small led believers to conclude that one person could not have played the part of both, therefore the manifestations must be genuine. However a more logical explanation is that Miss Wood had more than one accomplice. With so many exciting and unnerving things going on, it would be easy to distract and baffle the audience so they would not notice if one of their fellows was not where he was supposed to be.

Miss Wood produced some astonishing phenomena. Her spirit guide, Pocka, made marks on photographs by scratching the plates while they were still in the camera. Some of the spirits dipped their feet in molten wax to make casts. The evidence, written by believers, sounds very exciting. But engravings of the results of these manifestations are extremely disappointing. In the early days of photography, plates were often imperfect. The wax casts have only the slightest resemblance to feet.

It's also worth pointing out that if Miss Wood was asked to do anything too unusual, the spirits would fail her. When asked by a society in Belper, Derbyshire, to sit in a locked wire-netting cage for the duration of the séance, Miss Wood agreed. But on the first evening, materialisation could not take place. The spirit guide informed the audience that because the cage test was new, the experiment should be tried again in two nights time. This presumably gave Miss Wood and her friends time to work out a way to overcome the obstacle. The second séance was a success. A few weeks later, two gentlemen wanted to fasted a velvet collar around the medium's neck with a padlock, tie a string through the collar and nail the string to the floor. Some of the audience were shocked at this suggestion, and Pocka declared that because of the disharmony in the room, the spirits could not manifest that night. However, half an hour later, Miss Wood agreed to wear the collar, presumably having come up with a counter plan.

# SKIN AND BONE

In the Local Studies Collection of Newcastle City Library, there is a book not quite like any other. One of its pages is made from human skin.

It's a macabre souvenir of a notorious murder committed in 1816. The skin is that of Charles Smith, the man convicted and hanged for the crime, and the book also contains details of his trial and execution, his dying speech and articles written by Smith while in prison.

Charles Smith was an Irishman who came to Tyneside from Staffordshire or Yorkshire. His first job in Newcastle was at St Anthon's pottery. He then moved to Dawson's pottery at Hylton Low Ford on the River Wear. Finally, at Easter 1816, he began working for John Dalton and Sons at their pottery at Stepney by the Ouseburn.

On 16 November, 1816, Dalton's pottery went into bankruptcy. The Sheriff's officer took charge of the premises and an elderly man, Charles Stuart, was appointed to live in an office above the pottery's warehouse, sell off the pottery's stock and take charge of the money.

At about 5am on 4 December, Jane Buckham and Thomas Passmore were passing by the pottery when they saw Stuart looking out of the window. He called to them:

'Alarm the people for the factory has been robbed last night; they have almost murdered me, and left me for dead.'

The pair rushed off to find the foreman, Mr Wilkinson, and some of the pottery workers. When they arrived, they found Charles Stuart sitting in his chair, covered with blood. According to reports, 'his head was much bruised and there was a hole in his head large enough to admit three fingers'.

The floor was bloody and there were papers scattered around the room. The desk in which the takings were kept had been smashed open and the money, £6, was gone. The kiln poker was found on the steps leading to the warehouse. It seemed to be the instrument which had forced the bolt on the warehouse door and it matched marks on the desk.

Stuart said that he had been attacked with a weapon so heavy it must have been made of iron. His assailants were two men with Irish accents. This immediately cast suspicion on Smith, and the constable and others went to Smith's lodging, 200 yards away in Stepney Square.

Smith was still in bed when they arrived to question him. Because of the quantity of blood in the warehouse, it was almost certain that the attacker's clothes would be blood-stained. Smith was asked for the stockings he had worn on the previous night and handed over a pair which were completely unstained. However, witnesses in the room while Smith was dressing noticed that the stockings and underclothes he put on had spots of blood on them. Smith had been seen wearing boots the previous night and his boots, too, had blood on them. There was also a bloodstained stick in his house. Smith explained all this blood by saying that he had killed a hen with the stick a few days previously, and some of the blood had spattered his clothes.

Smith was brought before Stuart, who was by then in a dangerously ill state. His skull had been fractured and the wound was causing pressure on his brain. He still managed to identify Smith as one of the men who attacked him, basing his identification mostly on Smith's voice.

After Smith's arrest, witnesses came forward who claimed to have seen Smith and another Irishman talking near the pottery on the night of the murder. One gave the time as 9.10pm, another 10.30, one said it was about 11.00, and the fourth 11.30. Surely only the most reckless of robbers would have spent over two hours in a public place making their dastardly plans. As Smith himself pointed out in his execution speech, because he had been met on the road at 9 o'clock on Tuesday evening, it was very hard to be charged with a murder which happened at 2 o'clock on Wednesday morning.

*The Ouseburn in 1899. Stepney, where Dalton's pottery was situated would have been beneath the viaduct, not yet built in 1816. However, this photograph gives some impression of the industrial character of the valley some 80 years before.*

Two of the four witnesses identified Smith by his glazed hat, though they admitted under cross-examination that glazed hats were commonly worn in Newcastle. Both of these men admitted that they only remembered seeing Smith after they heard of his arrest.

Much of the evidence at Smith's trial was similarly circumstantial. A pottery labourer came forward to declare that Smith had borrowed the kiln poker a couple of days before the murder. He said at the time he wanted to prepare his fire in case the pottery began working again. The defence asserted that this could well have been true, and would be the proper action for a conscientious worker.

A great deal was made of the bloody stick and stockings. They were produced in court. A reporter noted that the blood stains on them were very faint indeed, something also remarked upon by the defence. It was clear that not all the exhibits produced by the prosecution were relevant. The defence maintained that if the murderer were wearing boots, he could not have spattered his stockings with blood, as his whole calf would have been protected.

# Assize Kalendar, 1817.

## A KALENDAR of the PRISONERS in the Goals of DURHAM, NEWCASTLE, and MORPETH, tried before the Right Hon. Sir Richard Richards, Knt. Lord Chief Baron, and the Hon. George Wood, a Baron of the Court of Exchequer.

### DURHAM GAOL.

JOSEPH STEPHENSON, aged 24, late of Burnley, Lancashire, weaver, charged with feloniously stealing from the dwelling-house of Robert Snaith, of Norton, one black coat, one pair of black breeches, and other articles of wearing apparel.——*Guilty, Death.*

EMANUEL SOLOMON, aged 16, and VABIEN SOLOMON, aged 15, labourers, charged with feloniously stealing sundry articles of wearing apparel, the property of Tho. Prest, of Heighington.——*To be transported 7 years.*

DANIEL MACKENZIE, aged 2?, late of Sunderland, mariner, charged with having on the 20th of Oct.

CHARLES SMITH, charged (together with another person unknown) by the coroner's inquest, with the wilful murder of Charles Stuart.—Com. Dec. 27.—*Guilty, Death.*

MARGT. SCOTT, charged with having, on the 11th January last, feloniously stolen one promissory note for the payment of one pound, from the person of Robert Forster.——*To be imprisoned and kept to hard labour 2 kalendar months.*

WM. FORD and ENOCK BROTHERTON, charged with having, on the 24th Feb. last, feloniously stolen one tin-box value one shilling, six promissory notes of 5 pounds each, 22 other promissory notes of one pound each, the property of Robt. and Hindmarsh Thompson.—*Ford to be imprisoned 2 kalendar months; Brotherton Ac......d.*

Conversely, if the stockings were stained with the victim's blood, the murderer must have been wearing shoes and the stains on the boots would not be material to the case. If, as Stuart had claimed, he had been attacked by an iron weapon, probably the kiln poker which matched so well the damage to door and desk, of what relevance was Smith's wooden stick? Tampering with evidence had also taken place during the investigation of the case. A blood-soaked cloth found at the scene of the crime was given to the constable. He admitted to putting it inside one of Smith's boots for safekeeping, thus raising the possibility of contamination of evidence. The poker found on the warehouse steps had been returned to its proper place in the gloss kiln by the time the constable and the foreman returned from Smith's lodging. Smith could not have done it, as he was under observation the whole time.

The defence made a valiant attempt to prove Smith's innocence. Doubt was cast on Stuart's testimony. The old man had been gravely injured in the attack. A surgeon at the Infirmary had trepanned him. This was a gruesome and delicate operation involving boring a hole in the skull in order to relieve pressure on the brain. After some days he fell into a stupor and had to be shaken into consciousness to give his deposition. Was he really in a fit state to identify his attacker? He based his identification on Smith's voice, yet there were other Irishmen working at the pottery. Could he have been mistaken? He was an elderly man who had been badly beaten. He was dying. Making his deposition must have a terrible ordeal. Two surgeons from the Infirmary were brought in to testify that he was so badly injured that his evidence was unreliable.

And what of the other attacker? Stuart and several of the

witnesses stated that two men were involved in the crime, yet no attempt seems to have been made during the investigation and trial to find a second man, or to link Smith with a possible accomplice. Nor was there any mention of finding the proceeds of the robbery in Smith's possession.

By modern standards, Smith had by no means a fair trial. Yet despite all the contradictions in the evidence presented during the six and a half hour hearing, it took only a short deliberation for the jury to return a guilty verdict. Smith was sentenced to hang.

Smith had been married for only seven years and he had two small daughters. His wife did her best to make sure he was comfortable in prison, and was as attentive as she was allowed to be. Because of her loyalty, rumours began to circulate that she had played some part in the crime.

The family was given false hope of a reprieve when the execution was delayed because of an irregularity in the way evidence had been taken. When the dying Stuart was questioned about the attack, Smith had been held in another room, so had no opportunity to refute the claims of his accuser. The respite was short-lived. Smith was hanged on the Town Moor, in front of a large crowd, on Wednesday 3 December, 1817, exactly a year after the crime was committed. Smith was 49. In his dying speech he once again proclaimed his innocence and asked that no one upbraid his wife and children because of his misfortune. He also requested that his body be returned to his wife for burial, but this was outside the Sheriff's power to grant.

Like all executed criminals at the time, Smith's body was taken to the Barber Surgeon's Hall for dissection. The religious

beliefs and burial customs of the period made it taboo to interfere in any way with the corpses of respectable citizens. The dissection of the bodies of criminals was seen as an additional humiliation and disincentive to a life of crime. It was also the only way medical students could study anatomy legally. The body would be flayed before dissection, and it was at this point that Smith's case became quite extraordinary. Instead of the skin being disposed of with the other remains, at least some of it was tanned and found its way into the hands of a private collector.

A Durham newspaper dated 3 October 1818 reports:

*An eminent collector and antiquarian of Newcastle is possessed of a piece of the skin of the late Charles Smith, executed near that town last year for the murder of Charles Stewart [sic], which he has had tanned and dressed for the purpose of binding a large paper copy of the murderer's dying speech!*

The eminent collector was John W. Bell of Borough Bar Houses, Gateshead. He was a respectable professional gentleman, a land surveyor who, in 1809, was appointed one of the Commissioners under the Gateshead Fell Enclosure Act.

For some reason, Bell never fulfilled his ambition to have a book bound with Smith's skin. Perhaps the skin was unsuitable, perhaps the piece was not large enough, or perhaps he couldn't find a bookbinder willing to undertake such a morbid commission. Instead, a sizeable piece of the skin is bound into the pages of a scrapbook. It is thick and brown, and looks more like an offcut from a boot factory than anything that could have come from a human body.

The rest of the book is filled with ephemera relating to

Smith and the trial. Bell collected obsessively. As well as printed broadsheets giving accounts of the trial, the execution, and Smith's last speech, there are newspaper cuttings, like the one from the Durham paper reproduced here. Bell has obviously gone to a great deal of trouble to secure some of the items. There is a note, dated November 1817,

**THE LAST**
**DYING WORDS. SPEECH. AND CONFESSION,**
OF
**CHARLES SMITH,**
Who was executed on *NEWCASTLE TOWN MOOR*, December 3d, 1817, for the Murder of
*CHARLES STEWART*, at the *OUSEBURN POTTERY*, near Newcastle.

from one of the surgeons who was present at the dissection, describing the condition of Smith's brain (at the time it was believed that criminal tendencies would be demonstrated by some kind of abnormality in the structure of the brain). There is a list of the doctors and students present at the dissection. There is even a note, dated 1807, from Smith, apologising for the late payment of a debt. Again this might have been added to the collection because of the belief that personality traits, including, presumably, a propensity to murder, could be discerned from the handwriting.

Bell has added hardly any of his own notes to the collection. The most personal thing in the book is a pen and ink sketch of a cheerful little devil sitting on top of a gallows. There is nothing to explain why Bell made this grisly collection. Most modern-day experts in psychology would find his obsession quite disturbing. Was he fascinated by the murder because he had some personal connection to victim or accused? Was it the collection of a man of science, hoping to prove, or disprove, theories about the nature of criminals and

crime? Did he, perhaps, come across the skin somehow, and build his collection to complement this gruesome souvenir of a notorious crime?

There is a parallel to Bell's collection in Bury St Edmund's library. It's a book containing broadsheets and other material, bound in the skin of William Corder who murdered Maria Marten in the red barn. The Corder case was far more notorious than that of Smith, partly because the identity of the murderer and location of the body was revealed to Maria Marten's mother in a dream, but mainly because of the extraordinarily popular melodrama which was written about the case. The play is still occasionally revived today. However the Corder case was about nine years later than Smith's trial. It's possible that the Corder collection, with its binding of human skin, was inspired by Bell's scrapbook.

Whatever Bell's reason for assembling his collection, his interest in the case lasted for many years. Pasted into the book is a newspaper cutting, dated 17 May, 1842. It records:

*On Saturday, and by adjournment on Tuesday, an inquest*

*was held before Mr William Stoker, coroner for this borough, in Buckingham Street, on the body of Agnes Smith, daughter of the late Charles Smith, who was executed on the Town Moor, several years ago. It appeared that the deceased has lived an intemperate life some time, and on the above day, having arrived in this town from Barnard Castle, she went to the house of an acquaintance, but after sitting awhile she complained of illness, and in a few minutes expired. A post mortem examination was made of the body, when it was ascertained that the unfortunate deceased died from natural causes. Verdict – 'Died by the visitation of God.'*

Agnes Smith was unlikely to have been more than 32. Charles Smith may not have been guilty of the crime for which he was hanged, but he suffered the full penalty of the law as well as the gross indignity of having some of his mortal remains made into a gruesome collector's item. Nor did his family escape punishment as the miserable life and early death of his daughter testifies.

*The piece of skin preserved in **Particulars of the Trial and Execution of Charles Smith** by John W. Bell.*